How to Score with a Woman

Marci Ronka, M.S.W.
and
Pamela Dannyluk, M.B.S.

iUniverse, Inc.
New York   Bloomington

How to Score with a Woman

iUniverse books may be ordered through booksellers or by contacting:

iUniverse
1663 Liberty Drive
Bloomington, IN 47403
www.iuniverse.com
1-800-Authors (1-800-288-4677)

Because of the dynamic nature of the Internet, any Web addresses or links contained in this book may have changed since publication and may no longer be valid.

ISBN: 978-1-4401-4981-8 (sc)
ISBN: 978-1-4401-4982-5 (ebk)

Printed in the United States of America

iUniverse rev. date: 6/19/2009

Contents

Preface

One of us is a trained psychotherapist and former owner of a dating service. The other is a behavioral scientist who has worked as both teacher and consultant in the area of interpersonal relationships. We've joined forces and written, for men, a basic primer which demystifies women.

There are numerous relationship books telling us "how to catch a man." However, we have found a real void when it comes to books written solely *for* men *by* women. This is where we come in.

Let's face it. Guys are basically clueless as to what women really want or need. They tend to view us as incomprehensible, alien creatures when, in reality, if they'd just follow some simple guidelines, the majority of women would readily respond.

Although we're social scientists, we're not going to bore you with charts, graphs and scientific research studies. Our professional backgrounds will take a back seat to the task at hand: getting you laid. This is not about footnotes — it's about foot massages. What matters here is increasing the frequency and quality of your sexual conquests. We want to help you land that first date and, if you wish, develop a satisfying relationship with a woman you've grown to care about.

Without charts and graphs, what makes us uniquely qualified to help you hook up? Well, beyond academics, we've consolidated years of no-holds-barred feedback from all kinds of women. We have interviewed and counseled countless of them about what makes them tick. We've gathered invaluable information from actually running a dating service. We are eager to share with you decades of wisdom, knowledge and insights in an easy to understand way.

From a young man just entering the dating scene to a newly divorced one who has forgotten (or never learned) what works with women, and to every guy in between, read on and score, dudes!

1. Qualities Women Love in Men

OK, let's get to work!

We're not as hard to understand as you might think. A little insider knowledge, a little practice, and you'll be on your way.

The first thing a man needs to really understand is that the fear of rejection applies to both sexes. She is probably feeling as insecure as you are. Even Marilyn Monroe once said she wished she felt "blonde all over."

A date is like an audition. The more auditions you do, the easier they become and the greater your chance for success. Even your rejections will refine and improve your game. For women, the male ideal goes back to the days of the caveman, where certain qualities guaranteed the survival of the offspring. These days, it has basically evolved into: Is he macho, but not a bully? Does he exude strength, both physical and emotional, and is he still able to show his vulnerable side? Is he self confident, yet not pompous and overbearing?

Our experience tells us that women really value the following characteristics in men:

Self confidence

Being a good provider

Gentlemanly/a Nice Guy

A great listener

Affectionate

Sense of humor

Self Confidence

Self confidence is not something one is born with. Regardless of the circumstances surrounding your childhood, you can gradually develop self confidence by setting tasks and goals for yourself and achieving them. Start small. Self confidence is linked to competency. The more you come through on what needs to be done in your life, the better you will feel and it will show.

There are also certain specific behaviors exhibited by self confident individuals that can easily be mimicked, such as sustained eye contact and a smile. Visualization – a technique used by professional athletes to literally "see" themselves attaining a goal – can be an invaluable tool in all your social situations.

For example, in the privacy of your car prior to entering a party, see yourself in your mind's eye actually entering the room. You stand tall and are smiling, people are responding positively to your energy. If you encounter someone you know, see yourself offering a warm, strong handshake, asking them how they're doing, and whether they know the host or many people there. When you actually enter the room, always remember self confidence can be developed. The visualizations you have done will have already created a road map in your brain, making it much easier to behave confidently. The more you mimic the behavior of confident individuals, the more confident you will feel and the more confidence you will project. Focus also on the person you are actually talking to.

Another important technique is to relive a moment from your past when you <u>truly</u> felt self confident. Your body will begin to respond subconsciously and you will project it. Self consciousness is, by its very definition, a focus on the self. If you are devoting all your attention to the person you are speaking with, it becomes almost impossible to feel self conscious. Later on in the book we will share certain techniques that will help you in all your social interactions.

Being a Good Provider

Yes, we know. When a man senses that a woman is trying to determine his socio-economic level, it is a turn off. However, it may help if you realize that it's "in the genes". It doesn't necessarily mean that the woman is a gold digger or that that is <u>all</u> she is interested in. She has been programmed by over 10,000 generations to look for a mate who could provide for her and her children. Having said that, the <u>worst</u> thing you could possibly do is to try to consciously impress her with how much money you make, what kind of car you drive, etc. It is a total turn off and screams insecurity. Allow this type of information to emerge gradually, naturally, over time.

Big differences in education, income and background do tend to place a greater strain on a relationship, so like the old saying goes, "every pot has its lid". Search for that lid!

Gentlemanliness – Being a Nice Guy

This is an area that tends to understandably confuse men. Since the women's movement in the seventies, women's expectations have become very individualized. Some love old fashioned chivalry, while other women are offended by it and see it as patronizing. A good rule of thumb is to ask. If she is putting on her coat and is obviously struggling with it, say something like: "Can I help you with that?" Then focus on her response. If she seems genuinely grateful, she is probably a more "traditional" woman. If she replies with something along the lines of "It's OK, thanks, I can manage", that tells you she is probably more of the "feminist" type. This method can be easily applied to door openings, to getting out of the car (or chair), entering elevators, waiting in lines, etc.

Most women agree that a gentleman does not:

Stare at other women in front of her

Curse excessively

Ask to split the check on that all important first (or second) date

Try to covertly "cop a feel"

Bad mouth former women in your life – such as "my ex-wife is such a psycho bitch"

Invite a first date to any social occasion that is not in a "neutral" setting – such as your ex-wife's condo, your son's frat party, etc.

A Great Listener

This is one skill that can be learned very easily. Good conversationalists use several really simple techniques to both draw people out and zero in, with clarity, on what they are actually saying. These will be invaluable in all your interpersonal relationships.

Use the "open ended" technique: When asking a question, stay away from any that evokes only a "yes" or "no" answer. You want the person to go on longer, in more detail and more depth of disclosure – i.e., greater intimacy. Use any opening line that lends itself to elaboration on her part. Examples: "What do you think of..?" "So, tell me about …?" "How do you feel about …?"

When you first approach her, just say anything! Comment on the environment around you – (for example, "Is this place always so crowded?") Don't feel the need to be witty. Just be pleasant. Besides asking questions, share short details that give the woman topics to run with.

Really sophisticated conversationalists will actually mirror the body language of the other person in order to produce a greater sense of connectedness. For example, she crosses a leg, and so do you. She leans forward, and you do so as well.

It's surprisingly hard to just listen, particularly for men. Really take in what is being said. For example, guys have a tendency, when presented with a problem, to want to fix it. They offer concrete suggestions which, although they are trying to be helpful, often backfire. For someone to be perceived as empathic, initially they must simply listen. When a pause occurs, it's very appropriate to say something like "I'm so sorry" or "You must have felt awful", or "Wow" or "That's great!" This allows the other person to vent while feeling they are truly being completely heard and understood. If, by the end of the conversation, you've come up with a suggestion you are dying to share, <u>ask</u> if you can offer a potentially helpful thought. By then she'll be more receptive.

When a woman is talking about her family or about her work, it is particularly important that you really listen. There are very few subjects (aside from her relationship with <u>you</u>) that are as important to her. By truly listening, you are showing that you are interested in her life. A woman can tell when you're thinking about something else and just pretending to listen. Trust us on this one. Don't look at your watch while she's talking to you.

Affectionate

A woman <u>loves</u> an affectionate man. No qualifiers. No ifs, ands or buts. Of course, we're not talking first couple of dates here, but if you two are dating … put your arm around her, hold her hand, stroke her cheek, give her a kiss. Women complain a great deal about how "sexualized" men's touching is and are really appreciative of affectionate, non-sexual touch. Men are far more "goal oriented" than women and thus sometimes confuse affectionate touching with foreplay. They are two completely different and distinct ways of feeling close.

Women are the ultimate nurturers and daily get to partake of the joys of non sexual touching with children and girlfriends. We are extremely comfortable with non sexual touching and love it … so, please us and <u>yourselves</u> and learn to enjoy a sensual, non-sexual experience (similar to a massage – which, by the way, we are <u>always</u> grateful for) that <u>doesn't</u> lead to sex. Who knows? You may have the best sex of your life that night!

Humor

A man who is able to bring a smile to our face is a winner. We're not talking about actual jokes or using laughter as a means of avoiding intimacy. It's really about trying to find some humor in adversity.

A man who can laugh at himself and doesn't take small things too seriously is highly prized.

Life is hard. Everyone has problems. It's how well you handle the inevitable challenges thrown your way that counts. A person can whine or, instead, can try and tap into the ironies or humor of any given situation. Which response would <u>you</u> respect and admire in <u>her</u>?

2. Hygiene/Grooming

At the dating service, this issue was huge! On paper, a man could have been an attractive physician, with many interests … yet maybe wouldn't use deodorant or brush his teeth.

The following were the most common complaints from female clients:

> *No deodorant.* Androstadienone, a chemical found in male sweat, is an aphrodisiac <u>in small dosages</u>! Play it safe. Many people tend to be oblivious to how musty they actually smell. If you sweat profusely, use an anti-perspirant to avoid sweat stains.

> *Dandruff.* Don't wear black until this issue is corrected. Several over the counter shampoos are effective and readily available.

> *Bad breath.* Gargle, use mints or breath fresheners, don't overindulge on onion or garlic dishes on a date (unless she is having the same thing). When you brush, also brush your tongue!

> *Long nails.* Totally creepy. Please trim.

> *Facial hair.* Most women prefer a clean shaven man. Trim nose hairs and shave moustaches and beards as they tend to catch food particles and smell. They also tickle and many women feel it makes you look like you're hiding something.

Acne. There is no excuse in this day and age for bad skin. Go to a dermatologist and get one of several available prescriptions. They work!

Fat and flabby. Shows lack of self control. Not sexy!

Overly buff. Ironically, it's a turn off, as it's sometimes misinterpreted as narcissism (unless, of course, she's a body builder).

Trying to hide baldness. No hair pieces, please! Consider shaving your head. After all, if Bruce Willis can be hot without hair, so can you. At the very least, don't try to disguise the problem by bringing hair across from below the ear towards the opposite side of the head. Obvious and pathetic. Also, unless you are an aging rock star, long hair makes you look dated or like a Mauri tribesman from New Zealand. If you can afford a few thousand dollars, you may want to consider hair transplants from a reputable physician. If you are over 50, please don't dye your hair jet black. (It fools no one.) Instead, leave some graying hairs at the temples for a more realistic, natural look.

Crooked or buck teeth. Have an orthodontist correct this.

Poor table manners. Follow your mother's advice:

> Elbows off the table
>
> Don't talk with your mouth full
>
> Use utensils from the outside in
>
> Don't lean down too far over your plate (You're not a horse)
>
> Water glass is the one on your right side. Bread plate is the one on your left
>
> If it's an upscale restaurant, find out what she wants and then order for her

When you're finished, lay the utensils across the plate and place your used napkin next to the plate on your left. (If you excuse yourself to go to the restroom during the meal, leave your napkin on the table, next to your plate, not on your chair)

Women love to see a man display a good sense of etiquette!

Clothing

Who said clothes make the man? We wouldn't go that far, but clothes are pretty important. What you wear telegraphs your socio-economic background and how you view yourself. If you look good, you'll feel good, so:

Get rid of all your shredded and tattered clothing (unless you're only looking for dates in the "grunge look" subculture).

Need we mention dirty clothes, particularly underwear?

Severely pulled up pants make you look like a nerd, as do too-short (ankle-length) pants.

We do not want to see your butt crack. Pull down your pants a bit, but not too much. Be cool, not gross.

Unless you're a Goth, avoid excessive body piercings and tattoos.

Nix sexualized T-shirts.

Too trendy clothing gives the illusion of self-absorption. Most women prefer a simple, somewhat preppy style.

Unlike polyester, natural materials like cotton look and feel more sensual to the touch.

Living Quarters (includes your car)

Going over to where a guy lives and finding it filthy is a real turn off. Clean up your place if you think there's any chance she'll be coming by. We like it clean and neat, particularly the bathroom, bedroom and kitchen.

If you want your date to be in a receptive mood when she enters your man cave, avoid:

> Dirty dishes piled up in the sink
>
> Every surface cluttered with electronic equipment
>
> Old magazine or newspapers gathering dust in a corner
>
> An unmade bed that looks like it hasn't been changed in weeks
>
> Dirty, wet towels in the bathroom
>
> Empty toilet paper rolls
>
> Visible porn, condoms, sex toys
>
> Turning on the TV, as it kills romance
>
> Instead, when she walks in:
>
> Have soft music playing
>
> Offer to share some quality wine with her in nice, matching glasses, preferably crystal
>
> Let your answering machine pick up (keep volume off, of course)

A final note: If you own a weapon, for God's sake hide it. You don't want her to feel like she's on a date with Phil Spector.

3. How to Thrive at a Party

If you pay attention, you'll notice that conversations at social gatherings tend to move through distinct stages:

A simple opening line

Introductions

Trying out topics

Exploring common ground

Separation (hopefully, having exchanged those all important phone numbers)

If you get invited to a party, go! You can always leave early, if you have your own transportation.

Try to arrive early at an event. It will be less crowded and, thus, less overwhelming. Force yourself to talk to several people, even if it's the same conversation, then return to the person you found most intriguing. If she is talking to someone else, join in <u>silently</u> at first and then try to contribute something short and positive to the discussion at hand.

If you end up talking to a girl you think you would like to date, for God's sake, follow through!! Don't just say, "It was nice talking to you" and walk away! Women are constantly left wondering why a guy who seemed interested suddenly lost his nerve and didn't "close the deal". Ask for her telephone number or you will be kicking yourself all the way home!

4. Where to Meet Women

Blind Dates. Men sometimes shy away from "blind dates". Let us set the record straight: Blind dates are one of the <u>best</u> ways to meet someone.

First of all, there is some quality control. Stalkers and crazies are, numerically, kept down to a minimum. Cautious women are less reluctant to go out with you if their friend set up the date.

Put out the word among your friends and co-workers that you're in the market.

Give it a chance!

The Gym. This is an excellent venue. Not only are you working on your own looks and health, but you could meet a like-minded woman in a setting very conducive to casual conversation. Visit several gyms close to home or work and "check out the vibes". If you see her struggling with a piece of equipment, don't hesitate to offer your help.

Classes. Of course, your choices should be largely determined by your interest in the subject matter. Your local college catalogue is an excellent resource. Having said that, subjects like Art History, Decorating, Cooking, Arts and Crafts classes are particularly favored by women. Psychology and Computer courses are also good choices. If you like the outdoors, try tennis. The Sierra Club also has a number of "hiking for singles" events. Need we mention to avoid "car repair" classes?

A word about cooking classes. These serve a dual function. Not only will the quality of your own meals improve, but you will be able to actually invite women over to your seduction den for dinner (and save money on dates at restaurants). Women find it cool and extremely charming that a guy can cook. Chances are they'll offer to bring either wine or dessert (which lets you know how thoughtful a person she is) and … the awkwardness of trying to get us to come to your place for the first time evaporates. Just be sure that:

the place is clean

candles are lit

soft music is playing

the food is at least semi edible

Organizations. Special interests clubs, political campaigns, chamber of commerce mixers and homeowner association meetings are often social (and business networking) goldmines. The mall on Friday evenings and Saturday afternoons is a wonderful place to meet women. If you see someone you like, start a conversation by asking her opinion on a gift for your mother or sister.

Dogs. Get yourself (or borrow) an adorable breed (no scary dogs like Rotweillers or Pit Bulls, please) and take him to "bark parks" or walk him in any and all public parks near your place. Show affection to your pooch and teach him a couple of tricks. Dogs are time tested chick magnets. Remember this – if a woman sees you are genuinely kind to animals, she is more apt to trust and feel safe.

Book clubs. Your local book stores hold regular meetings where people read a particular work, usually a best seller, and discuss it. If nothing else, it will improve your vocabulary, always a plus.

Bars. A simple "Hi, what's your name?" while smiling pleasantly (not looking at her breasts, but at her eyes) is all that is really required. Avoid convoluted and clichéd lines that can appear rehearsed or lifted from a magazine. Remember, if she says "Yes" to a drink, don't flirt with the waitress and look around at the other 19 women present!

If you see a woman you'd like to meet, have the bartender deliver another of whatever it is she's already drinking. If it is a house wine, upgrade it to a higher quality. Smile a bit at her as she accepts it. Let her get used to the idea of an interested stranger before approaching her. After a few minutes, go up to her and just introduce yourself. But don't bother doing so if she didn't accept the drink or didn't smile back at you as she drank it.

Bars tend to be quieter than clubs and, thus, are more conducive to beginning a conversation. You can go alone (just don't let on *that* you're looking to meet women) and casually say something like: "I've been working on a project and needed a break." You can go with a buddy who is nice and not obnoxious. (Just don't go with a whole pack, unless you split up in twos.) In this situation, if you see someone you like and she's with a girlfriend, he approaches the other girl so your path is clear.

Speed Dating events. A practical option where you basically play musical chairs as you meet woman after woman, usually for two minutes each. It quickly tells the two of you if there is chemistry. Check out your local speed dating opportunities on the Internet. They're very popular in larger cities.

5. Internet Dating

The choices of internet dating services have tripled since the late 1990's, with consumers spending about $700 million annually on dating sites!

Online dating is an inexpensive, convenient and increasingly popular way to meet people. Another option is "video dating". In either case, in the world of hooking up, one picture is indeed worth a thousand words. (In video dating, you can't be fooled by photographs a decade old! So, if you want to try it, and can afford it, it may be worth your while.) Online is far better than newspaper personal ads, since hotter women who are confident of their appearance aren't shy about showing you their picture.

Online dating pointers

An updated photograph is your most important tool. Why set yourself up to be shot down? A picture where you look your best, but still look like you, is a must. There is nothing worse than visibly disappointing someone when you meet them in person because you tried to pretend you were younger or thinner. Don't wear sunglasses, as she'll wonder what you're hiding.

You don't want to spend three months with someone on line, only to find out, when you finally meet, that there is little or no chemistry. If you are intrigued with each other, try to arrange meeting in person as soon as either of you can manage it.

Don't lie about your educational background, what you do for a living, etc. It is bound to backfire.

Stick to realistic driving distances. To connect to someone you need to get on a plane to see rarely works out. You need to see people often to really know each other.

Try not to argue on line. If you haven't even met yet and are already fighting … that tells you that you are not a match.

The sound of someone's voice is very important, so talk on the phone prior to meeting in person.

Suggest meeting in the daytime at a local place. Women appreciate a safe, "neutral" environment on a first date.

Be on time!

Remember not to go on and on about your ex, your kids, your work, etc.

Listen to her, rather than focusing solely on the visual. You may find her smart and charming and might want to give her a second chance.

When on line, the less detailed a description, the more intriguing. Save the specifics until she has replied.

Go for intelligent, funny, pleasant and real. If you have to get off, don't be abrupt (i.e., "gotta go", "later")! Say something like: "I have to get off now. Could we talk again tomorrow?"

If you can tell she's not for you, be compassionate and helpful. Tell her that you wish her the best and mention something you liked about her. Do your bit to elevate the dialogue!

Finally, if you like this girl, show respect. If you save the sexual advances for the second date, she will be intrigued and tend to believe that you're after "more than just one thing."

The Sites

Match.com is an old time favorite site to meet people. It is even launching a new mobile dating service that allows its 15 million members to access each others' profiles and send messages to potential matches from their phones.

It is a large, diverse, well thought of site. We have been told numerous times that it is considered the best. Another factor in its favor is how easy it is to end your membership. They give you your money back, without giving you grief.

E-Harmony.com has an intense application that involves many questions to determine a particular personality type. It delves deeply into the psychology of each member. It takes a couple of hours to actually sign up (given its lengthy application), but many people swear by this site, which apparently makes a serious attempt at compatibility.

Another dating site, CupidsArrow.com, costs about $2,000 a year to join. It also has an extensive application process, however, expect to get a level of individual attention (way beyond interests and demographics) not matched by the larger companies. If upper class, quality women are your thing <u>and</u> you can afford it, this might be a company to explore.

If finances are an issue in terms of signing up … Craigslist.com saw 2.6 million personal ads posted in one month alone and is an inexpensive alternative. Plentyoffish.com, a <u>free</u> dating site, is also an option.

Numerous Jewish women have mentioned how successful Jdate. com (a predominantly Jewish dating site) has been for them. The actual application gears its questioning towards the religious, so we recommend it for those who prefer to stay within their faith. No problems reported with refunds either!

MeetMoi.com is a new mobile dating service to check out. You send a text message about yourself with your zip code number and, within minutes, your phone can receive the profile and text number of a woman who happens to be nearby. It's instant connections and becoming an increasingly popular way to meet new people on the spur of the moment. Meetmoi.com makes its matches without divulging members' locations to each other. Its services, based on location, are more likely to appeal to users in dense urban areas, where the dating pool is bound to be larger and more concentrated.

Some, however, have a complicated sign-up process. While many services will work across most phones, they often require the users to sign up for a mobile Internet data plan. Some carriers may block some services—or features of services—like sending profile pictures, because they consume too much traffic. And pricing plans still vary widely, with some services charging per text message and others charging subscription fees.

Zogo, owned by Wireless Introduction Network, Inc., of Englewood, NJ, connects users who want to talk by phone. Users who log in through the browser in their mobile phone will see a list of matches based on information they have provided about their preferences. If one of the match gets a member's interest, he can request a phone conversation, prompting Zogo to send a text message to the match's phone. If the recipient says yes, Zogo calls both phones simultaneously, without disclosing either member's phone number. Many young women like this system due to the anonymity factor.

If You're Under 30

It's really important that you get on either "Facebook" or "MySpace". Some go on both! The differences are subtle, but they are there.

Facebook

Private school kids

Private college types

Politically more liberal

MySpace

More blue collar

State university kids

More conservative politically

Whichever you choose, don't be too "out there"! Anyone for years to come , including potential employers and "significant others", will have access to your site and it could present problems. (In a number of cases, it already has.)

A warning <u>every</u> twentysomething we spoke to stressed is that these sites are real "time suckers" – i.e., you expect to be on for one hour and three hours later you're still on line. Exercise self restraint.

There are literally dozens of on line dating sites to explore! Having said that, meeting someone <u>in</u> <u>person</u>, at either an event or via an introduction, is still the more effective way to go. Get out of your bubble.

6. Chemistry

Social psychologists have been trying to determine the nature of "chemistry" since time immemorial. The only thing you need know is that it is either there or it isn't.

Another truism is that the state of infatuation tends not to last longer than about 18 months. The more reason to have a potential mate also be a best friend with many interests in common. Opposites may attract but, in the long run, extreme opposites don't make good matches. Common interests, attitudes and values help ensure long-term compatibility.

There are numerous factors, besides chemistry, which are mostly absolutes. You may just not be her "type" in terms of such things as age, hair color and overall image. She could have a boyfriend, be gay or have issues that get in the way of real availability. At a subconscious level, you may simply remind her of someone who has negatively impacted her life.

There can be so many factors outside your control that the best thing to do is to adopt a healthy, philosophical approach and move on. Keep in mind that there are about 50 million single women in the United States! There are sure to be a number of women who would be perfect fits for you!

7. First Date Pointers

If you've just met someone, it might be more prudent if you ask her to join you on some <u>short</u> term activity you enjoy. Dinner at a fine restaurant could turn into an interminable (and expensive) waste if you two don't click. However, a drink or a latte at Starbucks, a movie or even a casual walk at the local farmer's market are some possibilities.

Ask questions! There is nothing worse than a guy who talks on and on about himself. It is boring for her and shows you to be a self-centered jerk, particularly if you fall into the traps of:

Using her for free therapy. Parental issues, problems at work, your ex, your delinquent teenage years, are all huge red flags as to the state of your mental health. Even if she is a licensed psychotherapist, don't do it. Keep it light and fun. View it as a dialogue, not a monologue. Your conversation should go back and forth like a tennis match.

Barraging her with your life story. By being interested in <u>her</u> and drawing <u>her</u> out, you earn major points and actually find out what <u>she</u> is about. We've already discussed the importance of really listening, so give her your full attention! If a particular issue is of enormous importance to you, you might want to steer the conversation in that direction.

Examples: Do you date <u>only</u> Democrats, or Catholics, or non-smokers? Determine <u>your</u> "non-negotiables" and <u>subtly</u> (this is not a job interview) try to find out.

Don't paw her. Unless she initiates physical contact, save it for the good night kiss. Then keep your tongue to yourself, unless you're invited in. Think sensuality not sexuality and see if there is reciprocation. If she lingers, you are in luck. If she actually initiates physical contact … need we say more?

Is eye contact sustained? Is she sitting up? Is she laughing at your attempts at humor? Is she leaning physically in your direction? Is she "tossing her hair"? Does she say yes to another drink? Does she excuse herself and come back with her hair combed and/or smelling of perfume? Does she agree with a lot of what you're saying? Even if she is playing it cool, all of the above give you a good indication she is into you, so pay attention.

When the waiter brings the check, you should pay. Do not ask her to split the bill <u>even if she offers</u>! She is just being nice, she doesn't mean it and it can brand you as a cheapskate if you let her contribute anything towards the bill. If she asks for a second drink, don't say "The Margaritas are sooo big here, let's just split the second drink in half." If that happens, guess who's gonna split? She is!

Always carry paper, pen or cell phone with you for phone numbers. Nothing kills the spontaneity of the moment more than hunting down something to write with. Make sure she has text messaging, if you prefer contacting her that way. Do not assume she has it. Most women prefer a more personal way of communicating.

Tell her you'd like to see her again, but don't go on and on about it or about how amazing she is. Be "cool", have some dignity. Ask as if you're assuming she'll say "yes", and project that if she says "no" it's no big deal.

If she asks you if you're seeing someone else, finesse it if you have to. <u>No</u> woman wants to hear you're in a relationship, even if you say it's a lousy one.

If you've told her you're divorced and she asks what happened, have ready a less than one minute prepared and memorized monologue. Don't call your ex a bitch, nor fess up that she cheated on you, particularly if she is the mother of your children. Just say that you "grew apart" or you "wanted different things out of life" or had "different values". Keep it as neutral as possible, aiming for 50% of the blame and you'll come off as a nice guy. Let's face it, whether you feel that way or not, consciously or subconsciously 50% of the problem <u>did</u> rest with you (that's the ex-psychotherapist talking).

It's not a bad idea to learn how to dance. We know, we know, it's not something that is a high priority in your life, but women love it. It can give you countless opportunities to approach women. If after a dance you ask her if she wants a drink and she declines, chances are (unless she's a member of Alcoholics Anonymous) she was using you as a dancing partner rather than wanting to get to know you better. Thank her and don't waste any more time. Move on.

No "downer" topics! This is a must!! The following should be avoided on a first date at <u>all</u> costs:

> Family issues ("I hate my mother")
>
> Your latest operation in detail (do not show the scar/wound)
>
> Your ex
>
> Generic anger towards women
>
> How much you hate your job
>
> Sex (of course this topic is no downer, but totally inappropriate unless she is drunk as a skunk and all over you)
>
> Death

Think about it. Negativity in general tends to negatively color human interactions and it risks having you viewed as someone to be avoided. This is a <u>social</u> connection you are trying to make here.

Aside from coming off as negative, also try not to look desperate. Think: warm, poised, confident, relaxed, happy, laid back and funny. Think George Clooney. Practice his little eye twinkle in front of a mirror. He doesn't get voted sexiest man alive over and over for nothing. Look at photos of the guy. He has raised the "aren't you adorable" look to the level of high art. A cinch to learn. Practice.

If you've practiced it, tried it a couple of times and it didn't get you anywhere, drop the "Clooney look" and just smile.

8. *"First Meeting" Subjects*

First of all, don't try to impress and don't criticize. Be an informed conversationalist without acting like a know-it-all.

These are some appropriate subjects for a first date:

Films

Restaurants

Travel

Art

Literature

Politics/Current Events (if you don't mind risking a little controversy)

If it's the Holidays, ask something like: "How do you like to spend them?" Notice this is an "open ended" question – one that doesn't require only a "yes" or "no" answer.

Sports (but only if she is fit and into it). For instance, if a particular sport is one of your favorite activities, ask "Do you play tennis (swim, etc.)?"

Avoid talk about video games, poker, etc., at all costs. Save it for your guy friends.

If you ask her if she has a boyfriend and she says "No", that is very significant. If she says "Yes" (which could even be a "white lie" to blow you away), <u>move</u> <u>on</u>, but nicely – she could be with a girl friend you really can click with.

9. She Gave You Her Number!

Congratulations! You obviously made a positive impression. Unless you were both really intoxicated and she comes to regret it, you are ready for "Phase Two".

It's very important that you wait a couple of days. Calling her the next day will make you look (here goes that dreaded word again) <u>desperate</u>. Even if you've been thinking about her and you two just had a fantastic time, wait. It will make you more desirable, like you are a busy guy, with an active, interesting life.

It is also crucial that you don't wait as long as a week. This risks her tagging you as a "player", involved with too many girls. She won't develop trust as easily, which is imperative if you are to progress to this second stage. If you've called her twice and she hasn't replied, move on. She is having second thoughts about having given you her number.

You need to understand that women are consummate game players. The #1 Female Universal Game is: "Hard To Get".

You're probably cringing right now, but, hey, it is human nature to value what doesn't come easy. Every woman has read at least one "How To" book on how to land a man. If there is one factor on which all agree, it is the value of playing the "Hard To Get" game.

From about the age of fifteen, every woman in America is bombarded with advice from friends and women's magazines on how to enhance one's desirability to men. We are told:

Make him jealous

Don't answer his calls right away

Do not, under any circumstances, accept a date past Wednesday for a Saturday night

Don't sleep with him on the first date, even if he's the sexiest man ever, or he won't respect you (probably true)

Be a little mysterious about your past

See if his pupils dilate when he looks at you (many women swear it means he's sexually attracted to you)

This stuff is pounded into us until it becomes second nature. All of this is specifically designed to drive you crazy and want us more. Several sessions of waterboarding wouldn't get a chick to admit she's used any of the above ruses, but we all have from time to time. Now that you know them for the ploys that they are, you will, hopefully, take them in stride. Next time you're buying some condoms at the drug store, pick up one or two of these women's magazines. They'll give you invaluable insights into how we think. If you're young, buy "Seventeen". If you're older, buy "Cosmopolitan."

Don't be afraid of answering machines. We know it's less ego deflating to text message, but there is nothing more seductive than hearing your voice and it shows confidence. If we're not into you, it won't matter if you ask us out by hiring a plane and skywriting your love for us. A "no" is a "no." Don't be a junior stalker. It will make the one in a hundred chance that she'll change her mind disappear.

Regardless of how you contact her, if you don't hear back from her in three days, it's just not going to happen. There is only one acceptable reason she could wait more than 3 days to get back to you: She's in the hospital intensive care unit (and, who knows, even then she might have a nurse call you).

It is an ego boost for some women to string men along whom they are never going to date. Why? They enjoy showing off to girlfriends about how sought after they are. If you can't pin her down to see you and keep getting told to "call back next week", <u>don't</u>.

Most men and women understand that weekend dating is far more serious than week day nights. Start during the middle of the week and work your way to Mecca: Saturday night.

Chances are she is <u>really</u> into you if you're dating Saturday nights and she wants you to meet her friends or casually leaves stuff at your house. (The latter is always a "test" to see if you freak out, which shows you are a commitment phobic.)

10. Potential Deal Breakers

There are, of course, potential deal breakers that ought to be disclosed as soon as possible. Persons similarly afflicted can be met through a myriad of support groups available through the appropriate medical and governmental venues. Do be forthcoming and disclose such matters as:

Herpes, HIV or other STDs

Life-threatening illnesses

Felony convictions

Recently divorced. You are an emotional, walking time bomb. Do yourself a favor and wait at least a year to start dating. During the first year after your divorce you will tend to automatically respond to women as you had to your ex. If your ex cheated on you, you'll think that that nice lady you met at the grocery store is going to cheat on you too, etc. True psychological separation takes a couple of years, so as lonely as it can get … wait. It is too easy to fall into a comfort zone that tries to duplicate what you had, not realizing you are doing yourself and the other person a real disservice. Take a chance and, even if is a little uncomfortable for you, be with only yourself (or go out in groups) for at least 6 months! You will get to know better the most important person in your life: you.

If you are merely "separated" … let's face it, the bond between you two is not 100% severed, so it is best to wait until that relationship is truly resolved.

You need to truly understand what went wrong. Accept 50% of the responsibility and let it go. It is also crucial that you deeply figure out what <u>really</u> is important to you and how not to repeat the past with the next person. Only <u>then</u> will you be ready to try again and get it right in your next relationship.

Any history of violence ought to be tackled via an anger management class. Your local hospital or mental health center are excellent resources on this. If you are bi-sexual, be "straight" about it, especially in this era of AIDS. If you are gay, embrace your sexual orientation. We are no longer living in the 1950's!

If you are jobless, or are still living with your mother, focus on getting some real stability in your life before even thinking about dating.

Men with small children, unfortunately, often turn out to be undesirable potential mates, particularly for women over 45. Chances are they have done their own parenting (or never wanted any children) and are reluctant to take on the job again, even if part time, no matter how much they like you. Your children need you anyway, so it is best to wait until they are older to start dating in order to minimize the upheaval blended marriages tend to bring. Second marriages have higher divorce rates for a reason: the stress associated with step parenting. Take your time. Don't start something that is likely to end in failure.

A lot of men try to quickly replace their absent ex with disastrous results. Men getting out of a long term relationship, even a bad one, have a harder time with solitude than women. They tend to jump right into another relationship before they're ready, so take your time. Your kids don't really want a strange woman in the house, anyway. They want you or Grandma.

11. She is NOT Really Into You If:

You have gone out half a dozen times and she <u>still</u> won't have sex with you. Unless she is a virgin and/or deeply religious, this is a huge tip off, particularly if you have been taking her out to really nice (and expensive) places.

We hate to admit this about the "fairer" sex, but if you are a nice, interesting guy we might just "milk" the relationship for all it's worth even if we <u>know</u> that we'll never end up in bed. We'll play the "good girl" for however long you let us get away with it. Remember, if she isn't spontaneously reaching out to touch you, she wants no physical contact. She may figure going out with you is better than watching a Lifetime movie, so don't get used – move on.

Another clue is if she avoids going to your place and never invites you to hers. Suggesting the two of you watch a great new DVD you just rented (not porn, please) is a great way to get her to your place. If she declines, is she avoiding intimacy? You bet! She is also avoiding intimacy when she never offers you a bite from her fork or plucks off a minute piece of lint from your sweater or … you get the point. If a woman can't keep her hands off you, she is reeeeally into you. We are tactile creatures, we can't help ourselves. We love touching, hugging, holding hands.

If we are absolutely OK with dating you only once a week, you might very well be one of seven. At the dating service, several "once-a-week women" were saving money on meals by a never-ending rotation of nice guys. One was even dating seven men she didn't care about at the same time, one for each night of the week!

Don't think you can't buy her. (It's hard for most women to turn down a weekend in Paris.) But even if you could, would you <u>want</u> to? If she orders the most expensive food or wine on the menu, it screams gold digger, so keep your eyes open (and wallet closed) when you encounter rampant materialism. If she suggests Dom Perignon champagne on the first date, watch out! Unless you are Donald Trump, it's a definite red flag.

12. Lame Excuses 101

OK. We've established that you're a little better than a Lifetime movie and that you do provide a free meal. Let's face it. If a woman is <u>really</u> into a man, he doesn't have to question it. If anything, he'll probably start being nagged about "where this relationship is heading" (usually by the third month). The following are tip-offs and/or excuses you should <u>never</u> fall for:

> She doesn't answer your calls by 11 AM the next morning

> The "I would have called earlier but misplaced my cell" excuse

> The "I want to just be friends" line

> The "I need my space" routine (unless you're the smothering type who calls several times a day and, like some paranoid, accuses her of flirting with everyone) – she probably just likes someone else better

> She flat out says, "I have met someone else"

> She wants to go out to dinner and a movie (again, better than sitting home alone watching the Lifetime channel), but is "too tired to have sex" or has an "important early morning meeting". Unless you know for a fact that she prefers her sex in the AM … don't be taken in. Save your money. Again, don't let yourself be used. (Unless you are into celibacy, which we guess is OK if you're seriously considering the priesthood.)

If there is one thing you must get from this book it is this: A <u>little</u> jealousy once in a blue moon (i.e., once a year) is flattering to women.

Marci Ronka, M.S.W. and Pamela Dannyluk, M.B.S.

Seeing prospective competition everywhere makes you appear insecure and neurotic. Get therapy. Now.

13. SEX

Thought we'd never get to the all-important topic of sex, huh?

When thinking about your favorite topic, here are a few things to keep in mind:

The average length of an orgasm in women is 17 seconds.

Most women need about 20 minutes of clitoral (or G spot) stimulation to have an orgasm. Some (rare) can climax in just a few seconds. Others (even rarer) can have an actual orgasm from nipple stimulation alone! And (rarest of all, but true), some women have never had an orgasm and are at peace with their asexuality.

There is a great deal of difference among women in our orgasmic responses. Interestingly, cuddling without actual orgasm is just as satisfying for many women. Some cultures recommend that a man masturbate himself to orgasm before being with a woman so he can "last longer" for her.

Most women are extraordinarily trustworthy. However, never believe a woman when she says she's "on the pill". A lot of women long for a child and/or feel this is a way to "hook you in". ("Shotgun marriages" all too often end up as disasters.) Don't be duped!

Turn Ons

Sexual responsiveness in women is a great deal more "mental" and emotional than for men.

Women are far less "visual" than men. It is rare for women to be as interested in pornography as men.

"Dirty talk" is a turn on to <u>some</u> women, but the majority, particularly those over thirty, can be a bit prudish and feel embarrassed by this practice. Save it until you know her better.

Many women are not big on oral sex. Sad, but true. They just pretend to like it. If she is giving you "head", be assured she is really into you and wants to please you. Most women, however, enjoy having oral sex performed on <u>them</u>. There are two exceptions:

religiously/culturally repressed women, and

women who take a while to come and feel too much pressure to orgasm. They tend to have difficulty being in the moment and worry that they are making you work too hard, which takes their pleasure away.

Aside from its obvious social benefits, the women's movement has resulted in a great deal of confusion regarding actual sexual roles. Even in this day and age, a large number of women are still reluctant to initiate sexual relations, preferring to be wooed and seduced by an aggressive, yet tender (yes, an oxymoron, we know, but we're talking fantasies here) sexual partner. Thus, the still remarkable popularity of so called romance novels.

The most important variable in a successful sexual relation is communication. This tends to take time to achieve. So respect her likes and dislikes and she'll be more "prone" to want to satisfy your preferences. Think sensuality, rather than sexuality. Turn down the lights, please.

The Progression

Don't <u>ask</u> for a kiss! After the second date, say goodnight and really go for it. If you feel her responding, slowly move down to the neck area. Again, if she seems to be enjoying it, try stroking a breast. Take your time! Slow and sensual is best. Remember, you are trying to <u>turn her</u>

<u>on</u>! If she pushes you away <u>twice</u>, go back up to the neck area and try again at some other time.

Remain in her comfort zone and <u>enjoy</u>. Remember that women just love to kiss and obviously she is just not ready for more intimate contact.

Once you have progressed to actual intercourse … If she tells you it's great, don't keep asking if it's great, it breaks her concentration.

If she suggests a move, be grateful, not defensive.

If she's almost ready to come, keep doing whatever it is you're doing. It's obviously working, so keep that rhythm going.

Keep that tongue of yours from becoming "Deep Throat, The Sequel". Use it sparingly, not too "surfacy" and not too deep – don't give her a shower with your saliva. Again, think <u>sensuality</u> first, then sexuality. This applies to both her mouth and her ears!! Same for oral sex. Don't bite her clitoris, please, unless you know for a fact she is into S & M. Also, some women have difficulty concentrating when they are both doing it and it is being done to them. When it comes to oral sex, start simple and progress in complexity and variety.

If you're young or just don't have much experience … go to your local library and check out actual anatomy books. Visit your local video store and rent some X-rated videos (no "threesomes", please, unless it's just for <u>your</u> pleasure, or she's <u>that</u> kind of girl). Learn the physiology of a woman's body.

Also, keep in mind that there is a small window of opportunity before you turn into "just a friend". DO NOT WAIT WEEKS to make a pass. (Even waiting beyond three dates is pushing it.)

And … a word on post-sexual etiquette, particularly if it is a new relationship:

Fight the desire to go to sleep

Don't pick up the phone

Don't read

If you're hungry, ask her if <u>she'd</u> like something to eat or drink

Give her <u>lots</u> of praise – she is soooo beautiful, sexy, smart

Cuddle, even if you don't feel like it

If she has implants (or needs implants), pretend you didn't notice

Vary occasionally your sexual positions. You don't need to become an acrobat, but interject a bit of variety. Good lovers know that the woman-on-top position allows us to achieve orgasm more easily since the clitoris gets more stimulation.

14. Are You "Dating" or In A "Relationship"?

You like her, you really, really like her. You'd go as far as acknowledge you're smitten. Could she be a "keeper"?

Of course, it helps if you have enough similar interests to make it comfortable, as well as a few separate and distinctly different ones to give you important time apart. You even like her friends!

Is she, however, a match?

The biggest factor differentiating women in terms of what they want and can offer in a relationship is the F word. No, <u>not</u> <u>that</u> F word. We're talking about the Feminist versus the Traditional Woman.

How much of a feminist she is will color every aspect of your relationship. And you better find out before committing to a woman both what you <u>want</u> and <u>need</u> from her. Yes, chemistry, values, similar interests, religion, socio economic background, education and even political affiliation all increase your chances for a better match. However, the F word will affect every aspect of your relationship, whether you want it to or not.

Here are some questions to ask yourself:

> Do you want an "independent" woman who wishes to continue working outside the home, even after having kids? How important is it to you that a woman contributes financially to the household? What are your beliefs regarding day care? Do

45

you want a traditional woman who expects to stay home with the kids, at least until they start school?

Are you willing to equally share in the household chores, such as laundry, dishes, etc., if you both work?

Do you view marriage as a 50/50 partnership or as a captain/co-captain relationship, where the co-captain has input but the captain ultimately has the veto power?

In the midst of the hot flush of romance, it's rare for men to think about such things. However, with so many marriages in America ending in divorce, we feel that they should.

In any deep relationship, there is an inevitable "power struggle" phase where any two individuals try to impose their wills (calling it "my point of view") on the other. The degree to which a woman is a Feminist will determine how much she'll push her preference on any joint decision within the marriage.

Discuss how she envisions your life together -- from where you're going to live, to number of children (or no children), to household chores and finances. How close are either of you to your parents and how often do you expect to socialize with them?

How does she feel about your "guy" time, be it your important yearly fishing trip and/or your deep commitment to those sports events that take precedence over any other social obligation? Do not assume anything! Check her feelings on all you deem important from vasectomy to that sacrosanct weekly poker game with your male buddies.

Another recent phenomenon that can be traced to the Women's Movement is the emergence of the female "commitment phobic". Previously only the domain of men, some women are now more reluctant than ever to give up their freedom. Independent incomes lead to higher expectations in a mate and the high divorce rate makes intimacy an anxiety provoking proposition.

Another factor, particularly in many women over 30, that makes us skittish is all those cumulative years of bad dating experiences.

It becomes progressively more difficult for a woman to behave in a vulnerable fashion (so needed in any relationship) when she's been emotionally pummeled by men for years. We don't want to get hurt, so we develop this hard, outer shell. Yet, underneath it all, we still hope to meet a man who is patient enough to break through this wall.

Sometimes you may feel you are being expected to prove yourself and … you are. Be patient. Be consistent. Call when you said you'd call. Avoid speaking of former girlfriends, whether they dumped you or you them. When a woman says tell me the truth, don't – unless you're willing to live with the consequences.

If it entails any question about how she looks and how she is dressed, <u>always</u> reply diplomatically. For you to agree with her that she is getting fat or is too old for a short skirt is an enormous mistake. Women want compliments and reassurance, not brutal honesty. If indeed she is getting fat, suggest a long walk after dinner because "it's such a beautiful night" and hold hands! Express an interest in learning how to cook and volunteer to prepare dinner a couple of nights a week. (Your meals, of course, will be low on carbs and calories.)

If she asks if you find a girl friend of hers attractive … fib. The perfect answer? "Wow, <u>her</u>? Give me a minute to think, as it's not something I've <u>ever</u> thought about!" Take a beat before arriving at the obviously correct answer: "She's certainly not as sexy as you."

You get our drift. Reassure us when you see us drowning in all our insecurities. We'll love you for it in every sense of the word.

You are no longer just dating. You feel you are now in a "relationship". But how can you really be sure? You've crossed that imperceptible line if:

> You are seeing her several times a week, including weekends

> She has introduced you to her family

> You know her friends by name

> You are having sex

You have a tacit understanding that you two are not dating other people

You know when she is having her period and can handle her PMS. (By the way, this time in a woman's life requires patience and extra cuddling, not to mention receptivity to talking about "feelings". Don't tell her she is being impossible to live with or being a bitch. She'll go ballistic and you'll be sleeping on the couch that night. The same goes for menopause. Indulge her, the payoff is worth it.)

You refer to her as your "girlfriend"

She leaves personal items at your place and it doesn't freak you out

You feel free to spontaneously call each other

You love her, have told her so and she has replied that she loves you too

We know it is sometimes difficult for a man to verbalize his feelings. Try it, you might like it.

15. The "Relationship"

Congratulations! Now comes the tricky part. Novelty is exciting, so to maintain and grow a relationship, you need to take a more active role in its nurturing and development.

First of all, in this phase you do <u>not</u> want her to take you for granted. Also, the sad truth is that no woman likes, wants or respects a salivating puppy at her beck and call. A little mystery and the occasional unavailability, even if just for a guys-only event, is crucial. As every magazine and women's relationship book tells her to, after a year of dating her exclusively, she is invariably going to ask where the relationship is heading. A little elusiveness might buy you a few more months before commitment or break up. You might want to try saying "Let's enjoy each other for now, give us more time." If, understandably, she is dealing with her biological clock, then don't string her along. Be honest, let her know your true intentions!

It's an interesting thing with women. On the one hand, we love affection and adore to be told that we are loved. On the other hand, we don't want smother love from our men. Not at this stage, anyway.

You also want to encourage independence in her. It is healthy for a relationship when the individuals have a life outside the couple bond. It makes it more interesting and dynamic when you do come together, rather than if you are always joined at the hip.

For a man, actually living with a woman is the best of all arrangements. You save money (since expenses are shared), your place is neater (as women prefer a nicer environment) and sex is available 24/7 without commitment. You're probably eating a lot better as well.

Don't be afraid to try it. If it doesn't work out, you (or she) can always move out. Just remember that after seven years, she legally becomes your common law wife, with rights to property, etc.

Evaluate during this time if she is truly a fit. Try and hold off making a formal commitment for a couple of years. You want to get to really know her and dispassionately assess if you can live with her faults (we all have them). More problems arise in a marriage from people trying (and failing) to change the other person.

Can you live with someone who is chronically late? Messy? A pack rat? Excessively jealous? When and how many children does she want? Do <u>you</u> want? How do you feel about her family, her friends?

By the way, try to find out from your girlfriend about her parental triggers. For example, politics is a perfect example of a subject that can unnecessarily create a chasm in your relationship with <u>them</u>. Also, did she experience <u>any</u> form of abuse from her parents?

We strongly urge you not to go away together for a weekend until you've been dating for at least a couple of months. You'd be surprised at the number of problems (not to mention the expense) of being saddled with a woman you are not compatible with for three days around the clock.

Gifts is an area that needs to be navigated with a little thought. We recommend neutral objects, such as sweaters and necklaces rather than lingerie. Undergarments are too sexualized an item and are best to avoid until after you're married. A gift, to us, is not about money. A small, thoughtful little thing that shows us you have been <u>listening</u> will get you further than gold earrings.

We can't stress enough the importance of what women ambiguously refer to as you being romantic. Anniversaries, flowers, cards, a surprise framed photo of the two of you, a picnic, holding hands, terms of endearment. These little gestures are of paramount importance to us. We see them as tangible evidence that you care.

16. Turn Offs

These turn offs should be avoided by all men of all ages from all cultures at all costs:

Trying to help solve a problem by giving advice and/or proposing a solution, rather than simply <u>listening</u>

Not talking about your feelings, especially after sex

Crude humor of a sexual or scatological nature

Sloppy/messy/dirty person or residence

Not helping around the house (particularly if the woman also works full time).

Not accepting constructive criticism, i.e., gets defensive and strikes back in words or actions

Being a pornography junkie (internet or magazines)

Being excessively moody

Making obnoxious comments such as:

"Look at that chick … wow! She's a 10!"

"Are you on your period? You sure are nagging!"

"I just broke up with someone and I'm not sure I want to get serious"

"I have 3 kids under the age of 10 … you like children?"

"What's your investment picture? Can I borrow some money?"

Quoting your Mom or comparing us to her (unless you're under the age of 12)

Calling us "ma'am"! Instead, call us "beautiful" or "gorgeous" – anything that has to do with the adorable parts of our physical, non sexual, beings. If the woman is over 30, call her "young lady"! We love that! Just don't call the ninety year old standing next to us the same thing, as we will think you're insincere.

17. Resolving Conflicts

Try to stick to certain important guidelines to avert escalation while fighting. Some are harder to follow than others, but merely being aware of them can help you to navigate the inevitable problems that arise in all relationships.

Avoid the Silent Treatment, in which one partner completely withdraws, sometimes for days at a time. It is one of the most devastating ploys people use. Some people may simply be overwhelmed by and unable to cope with escalating conflict and anger. Is that something you are willing to live with? Try to engage the other person! In the long term, even an argument is preferable to complete disengagement. If she consciously (or subconsciously) shies away from a spirited give and take, is that a plus for you, or a minus? Do you prefer an all-out fight (and perhaps an erotically charged make-up afterwards) or do you want things to remain placid and calm at all costs? These are different conflict-coping styles, one no better than the other, aside from your own preference and comfort level.

In college psychology courses, you learn that anger is masked sadness (which is, underneath it all, a yearning for love and acceptance). Ask yourself and/or your partner what is <u>really</u> going on. Go deeper in a calm manner. Chances are you'll move beyond the symptom to the real source of the problem. This is always the first step in conflict resolution: <u>identify the real problem</u>. When a woman calls you insensitive, she means you are acting like you don't care. Chances are her feelings are hurt. Tap into that.

Once you identify the problem, <u>stick to the actual subject!</u> To digress from the problem at hand, throwing all kinds of past hurts into the mix, just makes things worse. Try to deal with each issue as it comes up. Clear the air. Don't accuse the other person. Instead, start your sentence with "I feel…" or "It hurts me when …". This allows the other person to feel less defensive and makes it easier for the two of you to attempt to reach a compromise and defuse the situation.

It is really important that you take turns expressing your feelings. No interruptions. Allow her to express herself and then take your turn. You might want to tell your significant other that you're going to let her speak for as long as she wants and that then it will be your turn. Remember, anger is masked sadness. Tap into the hurt that lies beneath in both of you. Things will go a lot smoother and you'll increase your chances for a positive outcome (such as, make-up sex).

Men and women are completely different in the way in which they try to make up. This point is crucial in understanding how a man's attempt to correct a situation often backfires. We all know that men are more reluctant than women to express their feelings. The whys of this are probably basic cultural programming. Males act, men are problem solvers, men are physical. This results in men trying to have sex in order to make up, to feel close again. However, to women, making out is not making up! Sex comes after making up, not as a vehicle by which hurt feelings are dealt with. This is a really difficult concept for men to grasp, so take some time to internalize it. Women need to talk things out first. Only then are we psychologically ready for sex. Yes, it's a bore, but that is how it is.

There is a technique that can really help anyone achieve clarity. You essentially repeat back to the other person what she has just said. By varying just a few words, the person not only knows that you have heard her, but that you have understood her.

For example: "What you mean is…"

"What you are saying is …"

"I hear that you…"

She may say: "I was soooo angry at her!"

Your response: "Sounds like you're really mad at your Mom."

If you want to carry this technique a bit further by clarifying more deeply what you have just heard her express, you can say: "Sounds like you're really hurt…" "What I did really hurt you." "It was really upsetting when…" Notice again that you are tapping into the <u>sadness</u> that lies <u>beneath</u> <u>the</u> <u>anger</u> and moving toward your true goal: a loving relationship!

We love it when you take charge during stressful situations, as it allows us to feel supported and taken care of. However, being a bully and constantly demanding that we do things <u>your</u> way is a recipe for disaster. Giving in doesn't take away from your masculinity, it just shows that you're secure enough to indulge us and not feel threatened. We want a strong man, not a dictator.

For both men and women, love doesn't mean never having to say you're sorry. It means having to say it earnestly, sweetly, over and over again until you just want to scream … and then (if needed) having to say it once again. We don't want a door mat for a guy, but everyone loves a partner who can own his or her mistakes.

18. Real Men Share Their Feelings

Sharing your feelings does <u>not</u> make you any less masculine in our eyes.

If you share your day, share your fears and share your losses, you'll get more love and sex.

It's a funny thing, affection. The more vulnerability you show and the less perfect you seem, the more appealing you become. Yes, women want to feel that they are taken care of, <u>but</u>, to feel that they are valued for their ability to <u>help</u> you? Awesome! That they can actually be there to listen to you and take care of you? Amazing. Open up! Do not fear it (yes, it is initially <u>really</u> scary), the rewards are incredibly worth it.

Anatomy of the Female Brain

Improving <u>all</u> her relationships is a top priority for women. When a woman goes on and on about an issue, rather than tuning her out and making it worse, understand that chances are she's really <u>not</u> trying to be controlling. Don't poo poo the particular issue. Allow her to go on and on about it (at least nod occasionally and maintain eye contact, even if you're thinking about work). You need to understand that a woman's stream-of-consciousness monologues are mostly her attempts at communicating and sharing concerns. If you're willing to sit through it, no matter how draining and annoying, she'll eventually wind down like a clock and you will have averted an unnecessary and unpleasant fight.

When she runs out of steam and there's a pause, just say "I hear ya". She'll pick up the cue that you have actually <u>listened</u> and that you deem her <u>important</u>. Her emotionality will start to die down. Only when she has gotten it all out will she be receptive to exploring different options. Something like "What do you <u>feel</u> (not think!) we need to do to make it better?" will earn you <u>major</u> points! Here, though, you <u>really</u> have to listen to her answer. If it feels right, say so! If not, think about an alternative suggestion and say "How about … ?" Listen again, without interrupting and so forth. It'll be more United Nations than Jerry Springer, believe us. Women are wired differently. Try not to take it personally.

Holidays, Birthdays and Anniversaries

These special days are cyclical markers or guideposts in your relationships. They are of <u>enormous</u> importance to women. Just take our word for it, these dates are HUGE! Humor her on this and she'll adore you! And, in terms of the <u>actual</u> greeting cards? … the sappier the better. Pleeease, no cutesy, jokey cards. Go for top of the line Hallmarks, with lots of pink and lilac hearts and poetry and pictures of couples holding hands and walking on a beach at sunset. You want a night of hot, scalding sex, right? Then buy her the biggest, most overtly emotional card you can, in good conscience, purchase without cracking up. <u>You</u> <u>will</u> <u>be</u> <u>rewarded</u>! Remember, Godiva chocolates, red roses and fabulous perfumes will also melt our hearts. These have become a cliché for a reason.

19. Criticism and Feedback

If you try not to view criticism as an attack, you won't have to talk a subject to death or get into a fight. When she criticizes you or is mad at you for something:

> Don't immediately respond ... first take a deep breath.
>
> Tap into our truism that <u>anger is masked sadness</u>.
>
> Allow her to vent. Objectively, ask yourself: Is there <u>some</u> truth to what she is saying? Is it a matter of interpretation? Is it something you've heard before? Is it actually something about yourself that you'd like to change, or is it just a part of you and/ or your lifestyle that is non-negotiable?

When facing criticism, we can all use some help.

So remember:

> Identify the problem.
>
> Negotiate an understanding or resolution.
>
> Let it go!
>
> <u>Then</u> have fun!

Some thoughts on the subject of compromise. To actually compromise in the context of a close, personal relationship is incredibly difficult to pull off. It leaves both parties unsatisfied and tends to build resentments. A far more productive way to handle differing points of view is to negotiate and/or accept each other's differing opinion without judgments. How? By negotiating we give up something and allow the other person the "win", with the knowledge that they will do the same for you in a reciprocal manner. Pick your battles and don't sweat the small stuff!

We're hoping we don't have to tell you how incredibly non-productive name calling is. Blaming her mother is also another enormous trigger for most women, as we have a near pathological aversion to being compared to the one who gave birth to us, so <u>don't</u>!

And, if there are children involved, you should save the drama for when they're not around. Don't risk an argument escalating in front of the kids, particularly when you're just starting to practice this stuff. Remember that fighting in front of children is emotionally painful for the kids. Don't do it!

If all of your attempts at actually growing closer from the inevitable conflicts that arise from intimacy fail, try the help of a professional counselor. Most couples don't need deep psychoanalysis (which is done individually anyway). Several sessions with a Behavioral therapist (or Cognitive therapist) experienced in couples counseling will give you a good idea whether the relationship is worth salvaging, or if the non-negotiables are too many and too conflicting to overcome.

If you've agreed to therapy, really participate. Don't just sullenly sit there like a teenager. It will be a waste of your time and money. Even if you don't end up together, the experience will tell you something about yourself and help you in your next relationship.

20. When "No" Means "No"

When you started dating and she pushed your hand away and said "don't", you tried it one more time and, if rebuffed again, didn't try it till the following date. Right?

Now, deeper in a relationship, if she tells you she "needs her space," call her one more time. If you get the same response a second time, take it for what it is and back off. Give her her space. She means it. Don't become a stalker. (However, if she needs that much space, it's possible she may be saying "I really don't want to be with you.")

Calling a woman a couple of times is an ego boost for us. Countless phone calls and showing up unexpectedly is beyond a turn off. We are all steeped in woman-stalked-by-a-maniac Lifetime channel movies and are terrified it could be happening to us. Of course, you're not a stalker and just miss her and want to see her but don't! This is the number one way to lose your woman forever. Have a little dignity, drop her a note apologizing and give her her space.

If, after a few months, you still miss her, you can call her once more. If she doesn't call you back, take it like a non-neurotic big boy, learn from the experience and move on. If you know what upset her (even if you pretend not to), don't do it with the next girl. If you have no idea what went wrong, do you really want such an uncommunicative woman in your life?

21. Your Image

In your office or at a party, try to copy the attitudes of the popular people. They tend to project outgoing behaviors such as smiles and high energy. Subtly start to mimic them and gradually do more of it until it becomes second nature. It may be hard for you to believe, but you <u>can</u> affect how people see you.

Marketing a product is very similar to personal branding. Write down in 25 words of less: What do you want people to say about you when you leave the room? You'll learn a lot from this. You really need to be aware how your behavior impacts others. The ability to successfully interact with all kinds of people can be developed with practice.

Unfortunately, it is human nature that if people don't know you, they tend to fill in the blanks with something negative. Make your best you known!

Conversely, if people know you, they invariably try to cut you some slack and give you the benefit of the doubt. On the job, it's important that you engage in "doorway conversations " – i.e., you see a framed picture of a dog or a kid in a co-worker's desk and say: "Hey, is that your dog?" or "Is that your son?" You need to try and connect with as many people at work and at social functions as you can. It's good for your social life and good for business, even though it's sometimes scary. Remember, everyone feels insecure sometimes.

Elicit and actually welcome feedback from people you trust, even if it's unpleasant. Don't get defensive. If a couple of people focus on the same specific things they find annoying about your behavior, maybe there's actually something to it.

When in a group, speak up!   In our experience, the couple of people who speak up first tend to be seen as more attractive and self confident (qualities we know women adore!).   So … speak up. You don't even have to contribute new information.   All you need to do is agree and elaborate a bit on what the person who spoke before you just said!

22. Women's Life Stages

There is one area of life that you cannot overlook when it comes to dating ... that is our Stage of Life!

It is so easy to get swept up in the moment when you first meet a possible partner. If you truly pay attention to the person in front of you, it is easy to realize the Stage of Life they are experiencing! We will go through each stage in a moment, but please remember to just be aware that this compass does exist before you decide to venture into a relationship! Even if it is just simply dating, you can be light years ahead of the game if you know the dynamic of the person's <u>stage</u> that they are in... Depending on the psychological and emotional background of each person, there are definite signs along the way that will allow you to make an educated decision as to whether or not you even want to begin dating someone.

<u>The 20's</u>: Look out, this is the time when hormones are raging and emotions are flying high! Guys, you are dealing with someone who is trying to "find herself". She is so up and down you may not know what will hit you next! There are a lot of plans changing and insecurities. They have just recently removed themselves from a lot of parental involvement and constraints (some may still be very much daddy's/ mommy's girl), so parents may yet exert a lot greater influence on her than you do. You have found someone with <u>potential</u> and that can be dangerous. You're probably at the same developmental stage that <u>she</u> is, so know that you'll also be a different person in 10 years. The biggest issue at this stage of life and the one that will affect every aspect of your relationship is ... <u>maturity</u>. If you're 10 years or more older than her, you may have to play "daddy". Are you willing and able?

<u>The 30's</u>: You have met someone at an age when she is probably ready for marriage and children. … Her career is booming, too! But … her biological clock is ticking, she is either obsessed with getting married or rather concerned … "Wow, I met a great guy, I really like him .. I could love him … his family is nice … yeah, I wanna marry him and start having kids! So what if I've only known him for six months!" So, look out! A thirtysomething woman is looking to settle down and have your children! And she was ready yesterday! Beware the stage that screams wedding bells and baby names. If she already has children, the pressure is <u>really</u> on! She knows that her marketability decreases the more kids she already has, and she'd really love some help (emotionally and financially)… and that means <u>you</u>. Objectively, this is the ideal time for both of you to settle down. You yourself have sown your wild oats and have your own career path on track. But, guys, if you're a decade or more older than her and have no interest in raising someone else's kids (or have never had children and don't want any), think twice.

<u>The 40's</u>: Hold your breath when you meet a premenopausal woman going through a midlife crisis! At least, she probably already had her kids, so you've dodged <u>that</u> bullet (unless you're now the one looking to become a parent). She is quite likely post-divorce, really on her own, and excited about exploring her independence and on a serious path of self-discovery. At the height of her sexual powers, she may date younger men who can keep up with her. So, if you're older, be sure you're up to the task! She has many outside commitments that don't include <u>you</u>, so don't take it personally. She's been hurt before, so she's going to take her time, particularly about introducing you to her children. She may not be as readily available for an impromptu weekend away and will sometimes not give you the benefit of the doubt, as she's probably flashing back to a problem with her former husband. If you can share her with her children (enjoy them, don't discipline them, it is not your job even if you end up marrying her, it is her's) and with her ex, if you're secure enough in yourself to treat her like an equal and you <u>know</u> you don't want kids, this is a woman's life stage that can bring you depth and the greatest satisfaction. Caution: If she has never married, this is a <u>huge</u> red flag. Take at least two years to get to know her. Most women

have been married at least once by the age of 35. So what's happened? What is wrong? You need <u>real</u> clarity in order to proceed.

<u>The 50's</u>: Peace at last … You have met a woman who is comfortable with herself and feels content with life. Most 50 year old women have arrived. The hormones have finally settled down. They are content with themselves, if they have done their homework and know who they are! A fifty year old may not have the most outrageous body any more, but they have an attitude that is awesome. You see, they really don't give a damn what anyone thinks anymore … and yet they have developed compassion and are more accepting of themselves and others. At this great stage of life, a man needs the maturity to truly know how to treat a woman. You cannot pull your usual games on a 50 year old woman because she can see right through you! If you have the power to handle a woman this age then go for it even if you're in your 30's or 40's. We hope you've done your personal homework because this is a woman to be reckoned with! You cannot get her pregnant, and she's usually more interested in companionship than in marriage. Remember she has gone through The Stages and has now settled into some wonderful wisdom years! She simply wants to enjoy life with you! If you are looking for someone who will have your children and prefer emotional moodiness, you had better look for someone younger.

<u>Post 60</u>: The same impulses for serenity and happiness are largely prevalent, though health and money issues during this time are more common. A woman at this stage might want a life partner but may be reluctant to get married as she can fear fiscal entanglements related to inheritance, etc. Having been a caregiver throughout previous stages, she might fear having to end up nursing an elderly husband in the future. Explore the stage of life <u>you</u> are in. Healthy communication skills are a key to any successful relationship. Be kind and give her the chance to trust you. Become the man with whom she can share her dreams and preferences. Read and take classes that help you grow as a person. Come to terms with past emotional problems that may still be getting in the way. Work on yourself to become a balanced man who has developed good communication skills and healthy boundaries. She will love you and respect you for your efforts. Realize that each of us

is slowly maturing into a place that helps us <u>all</u> evolve in the game of life!

23. In Their Own Words, Women Tell Us What Works (and What Doesn't)

"He was funny, sexy, smart and nice. We had chemistry and more. One evening he asked me if I would accompany him to an amazing spa. I was so excited, I told all my friends about the upcoming weekend. He called me several times to confirm the event and said it was a gift of love to me. One evening while having dinner I asked him, 'I feel so lucky to be with a guy as sweet and generous as you are! This spa is considered a very expensive place.' He said 'No problem. Since we're splitting it in half, my credit card won't get maxed out.' I looked at him and began to hear little birds go... 'cheap...cheap..cheap'... and realized the gift was a Dutch treat, a tacky move that ended my respect for him and our connection!"

Charlene

"He was so sweet that, at first, I blocked out his poor grooming. But, by dessert, I wanted to run away as fast as I could! I clearly couldn't be with a man like this. If a guy wants to attract women, he's got to pay attention to his physical appearance. I didn't want to hurt his feelings, so the next day I e-mailed him and said, 'Thank you for a lovely date, but I don't really feel the chemistry!' "

Jean

"On our first date, he said 'Wow, you look like a movie star!' He took me to a wonderful restaurant and we had a great time. He seemed very attentive, and completely taken by me! I felt so delighted to meet a guy who made me feel I was the only girl in the restaurant! We immediately began seeing each other. Each date was more creative than the previous one. He really did his homework and when I asked 'What are you looking for in a woman?' he said 'Do you have a mirror?', and then reflected the mirror to my face! Needless to say, we are still together."

Donna

"The deal breaker was the complexity of his divorce and the negative way he spoke about his ex-wife. Although he called me many times to continue the relationship, I told him he was a great guy in many ways, but that I just felt he wasn't for me. Show up with a healthy attitude!"

Celia

"He really listens to me, doesn't look annoyed or just tells me what I should do."

Joan

"We'll be talking and he'll just stroke my cheek."

Wendy

"Football, baseball, basketball … soooo boring. I hate it when he just sits in front of the TV watching this stuff and getting fat."

Kathy

"Video games at age 30? Is he an adult or still in elementary school?"

Tiffany

"We'll double date and he'll just talk to the other guy, like us women are invisible."

Dina

"I'm pissed off about something and he just refuses to talk about it, just withdraws … drives me crazy!"

Leila

"He's been having a problem getting an erection and refuses to even discuss Viagra with his own doctor. I think he's just too embarrassed so he does nothing, and I'm expected to pretend everything is OK. He hasn't tried to make love in over 6 months."

Sheila

"He's having trouble at work so he gets all stressed out and takes it out on me instead of sharing what's bugging him"

Marlene

"I tried calling him and don't hear from him for over a week, then he calls me with some lame excuse about having misplaced his cell phone. Does he think I'm an idiot?"

Cindy

"Almost 20 years later and I still remember how he cooked for me on our first date. I could tell he'd gone to a lot of trouble and I just thought, here is a great guy who could be a keeper!"

Susan

"When you're trying to have a serious discussion and they're staring at your breasts, what a turn off!"

Lynn

"I was six months pregnant and he was accusing me of flirting with the 'Baby Proofing' technician!"

Adriane

"When we got engaged he told me he didn't care if our kids were raised Catholic, but now just taking them to Mass on Sundays is a problem."

Kelly

"I work all day and I'm <u>still</u> expected to do all the housework while he relaxes online."

Sandee

"After I broke up with this guy, he kept calling me at all hours of the night! He wouldn't say anything, but I knew it was him, I could hear him trying to breathe through his allergies. It was like some grade B horror flick."

Eleanor

"After our divorce, I thought the courts had pretty much spelled out how we would co-parent. But he fights me on every little thing and doesn't give a damn how the kids are being affected by all of this."

Bobbie

"When I wanted to end my membership on Match.com, it only took me five minutes and they were very gracious."

Pam

"Meeting Jewish guys is really important to me, so JDate.com is great!"

Eva

"I'm at a party and this geeky, balding guy with thick glasses comes over. I say to myself, 'Oh, God, here we go again!' and get ready to ditch him. Well, he had this wonderful, self-deprecating sense of humor! Starts to tell me about the TV show 'Beauty and the Geek', and sort of comparing it to us … To make a long story short, we've been dating steadily for 6 months."

Kimmie

"He brings me silly little gifts just 'cause he loves me."

Cynthia

"On my first year anniversary, I got a blender. Welcome to marriage."

Sue

"Tell us often that you love us … and show it."

Marci and Pamela

24. Afterword

Beyond hooking up, we <u>all</u> want an emotional connection. We <u>all</u> want to feel loved and to be able to love back. We <u>all</u> want to make our time on this earth as interesting, as productive, as rewarding and as fun as possible. Yes, you can be happy alone, but having a mate to share life's ups and downs enhances the journey and has been shown again and again to lead to a longer, healthier and happier life.

We are <u>all</u>, regardless of our sex, more alike than you might think. We <u>all</u> want to meet that special someone. Believe that you have something to offer to the <u>right</u> person. Yes, you will risk the inevitable rejections that come along in the search for that special relationship, but it's worth it. Remember, the more women you ask out, the better you will get at it. The unavoidable rejections will initially hurt, but, eventually, you'll accept them as part of the process. All successful salespeople know they have to endure a number of "no's" before they get to that gratifying "yes"! As in sales, finding your romantic partner is a numbers game. Keep trying, especially now that you know so much more about what works and what doesn't.

Develop your own best qualities and give others the benefit of the doubt. Practice the suggestions and advice we have offered you. We know you will become more successful at dating and, ultimately, at finding that special woman.

Know that you are growing every day in ways that maximize your chances for success. Believe in yourself. We know that you can do it. Go for it!

About the Authors

Marci Ronka earned her M.S.W from Tulane University. She has been published in Psychology Today magazine and lectured at the American Psychological Association's national convention. After working as a psychotherapist, she ran a successful dating service company in California.

Pamela Dannyluk is a trained behavioral scientist and has worked as both teacher and consultant. After her divorce, she began dating via "blind dates," classes, and the Internet. For this book, she extensively interviewed dozens of single women regarding their dating experiences.